Mind Reading

Kayla!

Paula Nagel

Illustrated by Gary Bainbridge

Routledge
Taylor & Francis Group

LONDON AND NEW YORK

First published 2017
by Routledge
2 Park Square, Milton Park, Abingdon, Oxon OX14 4RN

and by Routledge
711 Third Avenue, New York, NY 10017

Routledge is an imprint of the Taylor & Francis Group, an informa business

British Library Cataloguing-in-Publication Data
A catalogue record for this book is available from the British Library

Library of Congress Cataloging-in-Publication Data
A catalog record for this book has been requested.

ISBN: 978 1 90930 179 5 (pbk)
ISBN: 978 1 31517 491 4 (ebk)

Typeset in Univers Light Condensed
by Moo Creative (Luton)

Visit the eResources: www.routledge.com/9781909301795

Printed and bound by CPI Group (UK) Ltd, Croydon, CRO 4YY

Everyone thinks I'm so stupid.

Stacie's a bit jumpy today...
Maybe she's not feeling well?

Course I'm sure. We're always on the same team!
Come on girls! Less chatter please.
Wonder why Stacie's acting so odd today?

But why didn't you call or come over and talk to me?
I did wave.
But I couldn't see you!
I didn't know that!

All the thoughts built up inside me.
She looked really mad at me.
Why is she ignoring me?
Everyone thinks I'm so stupid.
I just know they're talking about me.
She's having much more fun with them than me.

Mind-Reading Workbook 3

Let's talk about ...
mind-reading thoughts

Here's Stacie to share some of the things she learned about her unhelpful mind-reading thoughts.

We all have thoughts running through our minds. Thoughts can be helpful and let us work things out and solve problems ...

I'm a bit worried about speaking in assembly tomorrow. I'll ask my dad to listen to me practise today. He can tell me what I am doing well and he might give me some tips on staying calm ...

Danny's not smiling at me today. I wonder if he's unhappy or not feeling very well? I think I will ask him if he's OK

But sometimes thoughts can be unhelpful.

In my story, my thoughts were unhelpful because they tried to guess what was going on in Kayla's mind.

This unhelpful thinking is called **mind reading**.

Look back at my story and see if you can spot when I thought I could read what was going on in Kayla's mind.

Draw or write about my mind-reading thoughts on the crystal balls below.

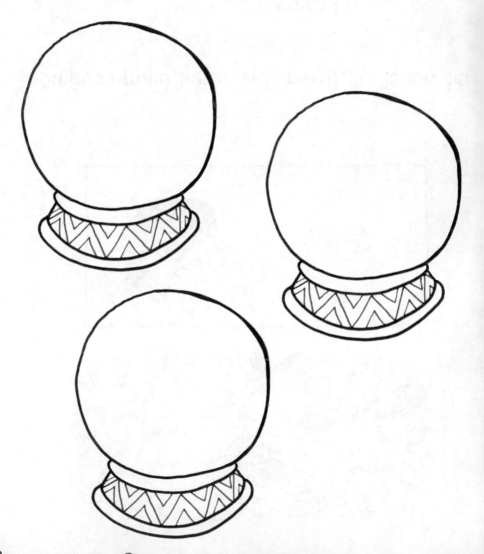

I thought Kayla was ignoring me in town when she didn't wave back.

I tried to fill in the gaps about why she was ignoring me, by guessing what was going on in her mind ...

When I tried to mind read, I got it all wrong.

Can you look at my story again and find out the real reason Kayla didn't wave back at me?

Mind reading often gets it wrong!

Can you remember a time when your mind-reading thoughts got it wrong? Draw or write about it on the crystal ball below.

Mind-reading thoughts often ignore the positive.

Mind-reading thoughts can be negative and take up lots of thinking space.

Mind-reading thoughts behave as if they are facts and not just thoughts.

Remember: facts are true and have proof; thoughts are just thoughts and may or may not be true.

Look back at my story and see if you can spot when I believed my mind-reading thoughts were facts and true.
Now make your own comic strip about it:

Mind-reading thoughts can blow things out of proportion, making them seem much bigger and worse than they really are.

When I dropped my book, I thought ...

Was this thought a fact or an unhelpful thought?

Did everyone think I was stupid? Look back at my story and see what Kayla was really thinking. Draw or write her actual thought below.

Mind-reading thoughts can make us jump to the wrong conclusions.

Was Kayla having more fun with the other children?

Was this a fact or just a thought?

Can you think of a time when you or your friends had unhelpful mind-reading thoughts?

Perhaps the mind-reading thought focused on the negative ... or jumped to the wrong conclusion ... or took up all of the space in your mind and blew everything out of proportion?

Draw or write about these thoughts on the crystal balls.

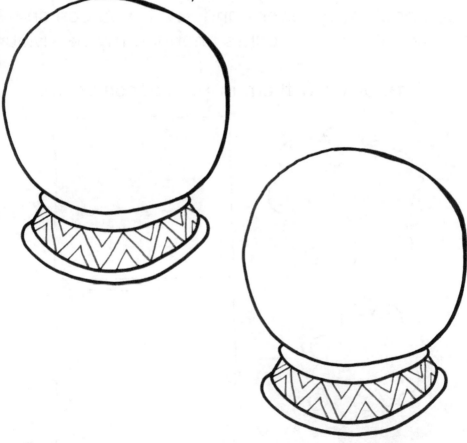

When negative mind-reading thoughts take over, our behaviour can change .

We might be tricked into believing that these thoughts are true.

Mind-reading thoughts can stop us from doing the things we would usually do.

But our thoughts can get it wrong.

Look back at my story and see if you can spot how my unhelpful thoughts changed my behaviour.

Write or draw them in the spaces below.

When I walked into the classroom, I thought Kayla was talking about me, so I didn't go over to join her and the others. I avoided them because I predicted they would ignore me.

Look back at the story and see what I did instead of joining Kayla and my friends.

What do you think might have happened if I'd gone into the classroom and spoken to Kayla?

 Look back at my story and see if you can spot another time when my mind-reading thoughts stopped me from doing the things I usually do.

Now make your own comic strip about it.

It's normal to have lots and lots of thoughts running through our minds. Some thoughts will be helpful and some will be unhelpful.

Some of the unhelpful thoughts might be mind-reading thoughts.

Let's think about what we can do to notice and manage unhelpful thoughts.

1 Try to notice your mind-reading thoughts.

Try writing some of your thoughts in a diary.
Notice when these thoughts are helpful
or unhelpful. Are any of these thoughts
mind-reading ones?

I wrote down some of my thoughts in a notebook
so I could keep track of my mind-reading ones.

What happened – Kayla didn't
wave back

What I thought – she's ignoring me

What I did – worried about all of the
things I might have done to make
her ignore me.

**Was this a helpful thought or an
unhelpful mind-reading thought?** -
It was an unhelpful mind-reading
thought because it made me worry
more and stopped me from talking
to her about it.

2 When you notice a mind-reading thought, remember to test it.

Ask yourself ...

Am I focusing on the worst?

Am I trying to
see into
someone's brain?

Am I blowing things out of proportion?

Am I
predicting
the future?

Am I jumping to conclusions?

3 Challenge your mind-reading thoughts.

If you notice that you are having a mind-reading thought, challenge it by thinking of other possibilities.

When Kayla didn't wave back, I could have challenged my mind-reading thought by thinking of some other reasons why she didn't wave back.

Remember to check out your unhelpful mind-reading thoughts with someone you trust.

Who can you talk to about your unhelpful thoughts? Draw or write about them below.

Try asking yourself ...

What would I say to a friend if they had this thought?

What would a friend say to me?

Summary

- We have lots of different thoughts running through our minds. Some thoughts can be helpful and some can be unhelpful.

- Sometimes our thoughts might try to guess what's going on in other people's minds. These are called **mind-reading thoughts**.

- Mind-reading thoughts sometimes get it wrong, especially when they focus only on the negatives.

- Unhelpful mind-reading thoughts can blow things out of proportion, jump to the wrong conclusions, and take up lots of thinking space.

- Try to notice when you have a mind-reading thought - especially if it is an unhelpful, negative one. Challenge your mind-reading thoughts by thinking of other possibilities.

- Ask yourself, is this thought a fact or just a thought? What would you say to a friend if they had the same unhelpful thought as you?

- Check out your unhelpful thoughts with someone you trust and don't forget to tell someone if a mind-reading thought is bothering you!